BEST KIDS LUNCH BOX RECIPES EVER

Healthy Lunch Box Ideas and Recipes For Fun School Lunches Your Kids will Love

Printed in the United States of America.
First Printing, 2013

Table of Contents

Is it a bird? Is it a plane? No, it's super mom! Here's a bird's eye view of what we are going to cover. I just know you are going to love it!

1. Little Fingers
Lunch ideas for the toddler

2. Fast and Easy
Quick thinking ideas with what's on hand

3. Make Ahead
Big batches to last all week

4. Hot Choices
For thermal bottles and microwaves

5. Breakfast
On the go goodness

6. More Veggies Please
Variety is the key

7. Snacks
Anytime yummies

8. Sammies and Wraps
Lunchtime one handers

9. Sweet Treats
Tasty finishing touches

10. Gluten Free Options
For everyone

Welcome Super Moms and Dads   2

LITTLE FINGERS
Bites and Bites   9
Apple Cheddar Muffets   11
Perfect Pizza Parcels   13
Shapers   15
Sausage and Veggie Rolls   16
Ricotta and Spinach Bites   18

FAST AND EASY
Rice Cakes with Sprinkles   22
Build a Nacho   24
Rollin' Rollin' Rollin'   26
Cold Chicken Noodle Salad   27
Panzanella   28
Granola Parfait   30
Salad in a Jar   31
Roast Beef Pita Pockets   33
Soft Chicken Tacos   34

MAKE AHEAD
Sundried Tomato Pasta   38
Glassy Shrimp Noodle Salad   40
Chinese Rice Salad   42
Chunky Chicken Salad   44
Pizza Muffins   47
Potato Pockets   49
Coconut Shrimp   51
Zippy Chicken Tenders   52

Grizadilla	54
Pizza Pinwheels	56
Crescent Surprises	58

HOT CHOICES

Loaded Potato Soup	61
French Canadian Pea	63
White Soup	65
Beef Barley Soup	67
Chunky Chicken Soup	69
Thai Spaghetti	71
Jambalaya	73
Manicotti	75
Tuna Surprise	77
Best Ever Shepherd's Pie	74

BREAKFAST

Egg Cups	83
French Toast Fingers	85
Oatmeal To Go Cakes	87
Breakfast Corn Dogs	89
Egg Paninis	91
Mega Muffins	93
Apple Breakfast Bars	95
Devilled Eggs	97
Bacon and Cheddar Waffles	98
Sausage Balls	100
Granola Cones	102
Pack a Punch Breakfast Bars	104
Squash, Carrot, Raisin Bread	107

MORE VEGGIES PLEASE

No Fry Potato Skins 111
Mango and Black Bean Salad 113
Gazpacho 114
Sweet Potato Tater Tots 116
Crunchy Chickpea Salad 118
Zucchini and Corn Fritters 119
Refrigerator Antipasto 121
Tabouli / Quinoa Salad 123

SNACKS

Zesty Cheese Straws 127
Cheese Crisp "Cookies" 128
Fruit Wands and Dip 129
Cinnamon Crunchies 130
Fruit and Seed Bars 132
Snackin' Snowballs 134
Sunshine Muffins 136
Popcorn Nutty Balls 138
Choco-Banana Flappies 140
Chocolate Energy Bars 142
Homemade Animal Crackers 144
Cereal Power Bars 146

SAMMIES & WRAPS

Carrot Salad Sandwich	150
Corn and Bean Pockets	152
Pulled Chicken Sandwich	154
Inside Out Sandwich Wands	155
Banana Cream Cheese Sammies	156
Ham, Cheese and Pear Sandwiches	157
Hummus and Veggie Pita	158
Ham and Mustard Spirals	160
Summer Rolls	162
Philly-style Cheesesteak Sammie	164
Buffalo Chicken Wrap	165

SWEET TREATS

Healthy Whoopie Pies	169
Karrot's Cake	171
Cranberry Oat Cereal Bars	173
Blueberry Cheesecake Bites	174
Healthy Oatmeal Cookies	175
Chocolate Zucchini Cake	177
Gingersnaps	179
Quick and Easy PopTarts	181
Chocolate Fudge Pop Tarts	183
Granola Balls	187

GLUTEN FREE OPTIONS

Chocolate Chickpea Cake   191
Coconut Flour Orange Cake   193
Orange Coconut Oil Frosting   195
Jumbo Muffins   197
Chicken Asparagus Crepes   199
Rice Noodle Salad   201
Tuna, Asparagus White Bean Salad   203
Coconut Curry Noodle Bowl   205
Chewy Macaroons   207

Welcome all Super Moms and Dads!

Hey there! So good to see you. If you are reading this (which you obviously are!) you probably have the same problem as me. Kids who may be smaller on the outside than they are on the inside! Where do they pack it all away? It is one of the great mysteries of the universe I am sure.

And on top of that, we (usually moms, but some cool dads too!) are responsible to make sure that the right stuff goes in. That's where Best Kids Lunch Box Recipes Ever comes to the rescue.

From the day a newborn becomes a member of the family, food is a huge part of the daily life of children of all ages. And until an age when they can really reach the kitchen shelves, add to the grocery cart, or pitch in cooking up a family dinner, our kids rely on us to provide the food that keeps them going.

Today, kids eat more and more on the go than ever. The school day, as young as daycare age, is a full day. Unlike previous decades (which some parents may remember), going home for lunch is very rare in our culture. And eating on the go is not just necessary at lunchtime. Kids have to grab sustenance before after school activities, for summer camp programs, weekend lessons, and even breakfast for those early risers who have practices or commute to and from school. Kids eat more on the move than they ever did before.

The bigger challenge is not just in finding food for children to eat, but finding healthy, affordable foods that cut down on addictive sugars, sodium, preservatives, and processed products that seem to get into so many kids meals nowadays. Thankfully, with a little creativity, and armed with a stock of easy to use recipes we can ensure our kids get the nutrition they need, in ways that they can enjoy day after day.

This guide will help sort out the problem of how to shop, prepare, store, serve and vary the foods your child needs to eat. Each section will suggest tips on making certain foods are prepared economically and transported efficiently. Hopefully, it will be just the tool you need to establish routines of healthy eating, smart choices, and an emphasis on fresh, local foods.

Little Fingers

Lunch ideas for the toddler

Toddlers love to feed themselves…it's one of their first signs of independence. When they are put into a social situation such as a playgroup, preschool or break time at a lesson, they will only eat if they are truly hungry.

Ready, available bite size food is the best way to go. Half-eaten sandwiches don't get wasted, and uneaten bite size food can be snacked on in the car or another snack time.

Bites and Bites

Make these the night before, or keep in plastic ware all week long for lots of snacking.

Ingredients:

3 whole grain tortillas

4 slices turkey

4 slices ham

250g container spreadable light cream cheese

8-10 cubes of cheese (medium cheddar, mozzarella, brick, Swiss, all work well)

3 dill pickles

6-8 olives

celery sticks

carrot sticks*

strawberries, grapes, melon slices, pineapple spear

Directions:

Pat cold meat with a paper towel to ensure it is dry. Spread cream cheese evenly over ham and turkey slices. Roll each around a melon slice, pineapple spear, carrot stick or celery stick. Secure with plastic wrap and refrigerate.

Spread cream cheese over tortillas and line with dill spears, then roll and secure in plastic wrap. Refrigerate for at least an hour or overnight, then cut into 1 " slices.

Plastic ware with many sections is great for all these little bites.

*Always buy full sized carrots and cut into sticks. Pre-packaged "mini" carrots are washed in bleach.

Apple Cheddar Muffets

These little bite-sized wonders are perfect for small appetites. Invest in a mini-muffin pan, and make up a double batch for freezing.

Ingredients:

Preheat oven to 400°F

1 very large apple – peeled, cored, diced (pear works well too)

2 tbsps butter or soy margarine

2/3 cup flour (mix of coconut, whole wheat, almond works well)

1 tsp salt

½ tsp baking powder

½ cup cornmeal

2 tbsps brown sugar

¼ tsp salt

1 egg slightly beaten

1/3 cup milk (almond works too)

1 cup sour cream

1 ½ cup grated cheddar, divided evenly

Directions:

Begin with a small saucepan and sauté the apples in the butter for a few minutes, then let them cool. Combine all the dry ingredients and set aside in a large bowl. Separately, whisk together egg, milk, sour cream and 1 cup of cheese. Stir into dry ingredients thoroughly, then add apple. Spoon into muffin cups and top with remaining cheese. Bake 20 -25 minutes, let cool.

Perfect Pizza Parcels

Puff pastry is one of the easy products on the market that speed up preparation time for so many simple creations. The hours it takes to make your own pastry could never measure up with the quality of good store bought pastry you can stock up in your freezer. Here's a favorite pleaser for all ages.

Ingredients:

1 box 397g- 450g puff pastry, divided and thawed

4-5 drained oil packed sundried tomatoes

¼ cup slices of pepperoni or other favourite Italian deli meat

¼ cup grated Parmesan cheese

½ cup grated mozzarella cheese

2 tbsps chopped basil

1 egg yolk

2 tsp milk

flour for dusting

Directions:

Preheat oven to 375°F. In a chopper or food processor, mince together the tomatoes and pepperoni. Add in the cheeses and basil and mix together, then transfer this "paste" to a bowl. Divide it into ten portions.

On a flour-dusted surface, roll out one sheet of the pastry into a 12" square. Cut into 4 , 6" squares. Fill each square with the tomato-cheese mixture slightly left of centre. Moisten edges with water from a pastry brush and over the right side. Press edges together. The bundle can be left like this, or use 3" cookie cutter to create a shape, ensure edges are sealed. Continue to make all the other 9 bundles.

Transfer to parchment lined baking sheet, brush with beaten egg yolk mixed wit the milk. Bake 20-25 minutes. Cool and store.

Shapers

Add a little fun to the sandwich routine with a selection of cookie cutters. A little cookie spray on each will help if you find the cutters are sticking to the breads.

Ingredients:

Breads - whole wheat, grainy, pumpernickel work well

Fillings – cream cheese with additions of: red and green pepper, pineapple, olives, pickles; egg salad, tuna salad, mince chicken salad

Directions:

Tips: There will be some waste of bread due to the shapes, but there doesn't have to be waste of the fillings.
Cut out two of each shape, fill and put together.
For a great easy-to-hold shaper, trim the crusts from a very soft piece of bread, cover with a cream cheese and wrap around a pickle spear or tiny gherkins.

Great for themed parties and picnics. Add "eyes" of pickle or olive bits, fins or feathers with fruit leather cut ups, and other crazy décor. Food is fun!

Make ahead and freeze.

Sausage and Veggie Rolls

These take a little more prep time, but are so worth it because they make a lot! The recipe scales down easily too. They are especially handy for making up when you have extra vegetables to use up or if you are in the habit of disguising vegetables for picky eaters. The ground chicken or turkey gives the rolls more flavor and they are packed with protein and fibre.

Ingredients:

8 frozen puff pastry sheets - defrosted

2 lbs minced chicken or turkey, or both.

4 eggs

1 cup quinoa or ground oats, flax (or a mix of grains to make a cup)

½ cup whole wheat breadcrumbs

2 cups mixed veg (carrots, celery, peppers, onions, peas, mushrooms, root vegs)

¼ cup chopped parsley

salt and pepper to taste

1 egg , slightly beaten

Directions:

Preheat oven to 400°F. Chop all the vegetables finely and add to the meat in a large bowl. Add in grains, crumbs, salt, pepper, parsley and 4 eggs. Massage together.

Spread out pastry and cut in half so a long rectangle is in front of you. Lay a long portion of the meat mixture along the bottom edge. Moisten the edges with the beaten egg and roll pastry over the meat, seal the edges. You should have two layers of the pastry over the meat, overlapping for at least 1 cm. Place the roll on parchment covered baking sheet and brush again with the beaten egg. As you make up all 8 logs, refrigerate while you keep working.

With a thin sharp knife, slice each roll into 7-8 bite-sized pieces. Lay on parchment and bake 15 min, then turn oven down to 350°F and continue cooking until browned. Watch the slices near the pan edges as they may cook sooner; just re-arrange the pans. Makes about 100!

Ricotta and Spinach Bites

Ricotta is such a smooth creamy cheese to work with but cooks up better than cream cheese. Of course, use fresh spinach if you have it, but steam it a little first.

Ingredients:

2 tbsp. butter or soy margarine

1 clove minced garlic

3 tbsp chopped onion

2 large beaten eggs

1 cup ricotta cheese (low or full fat)

½ cup grated Parmesan cheese

½ cup shredded mozzarella cheese

1 10 oz pkg defrosted drained, squeezed, chopped spinach

½ tsp sea salt

Directions:

Preheat oven to 350°F. Saute onion and garlic in melted butter and then let cool. Meanwhile whisk the eggs, stir I the cheeses, and then the spinach and salt. Add in the onion and garlic. Pour mixture into well-greased mini muffin cups.
Bake 20 -25 minutes. Cool. Store in airtight container.

Fast & Easy

Quick thinking ideas
with what's on hand

If you stock your pantry and fridge with plenty of "go to" items, you'll amaze yourself with the quick nutritious options you can put together. Today, there are so many varieties of ready available foods, from all over the world. No brown bag has to suffer with a quickly slapped together white bread PB&J, apple and cookie anymore!

Rice Cakes with Sprinkles

These are colorful and fun to prepare. And rice cakes come in many flavors so use your imagination. When you pack two together as a sandwich, they can easily be pulled apart to be eaten separately, each with their own topping. Kids love to play with their food!

Ingredients:

For each pair:

2 rice cakes

2 tbsps softened cream cheese

1/8 tsp cinnamon

2-3 tbsps. mixed dried fruit (raisins, pineapple, apricots, cranberries)

...savory version...

2 rice cakes in cheese or dill flavor

2 tbsps softened cream cheese

dash of garlic salt, parsley and pepper

2-3 tbsps veg (peppers, celery, sundried tomato, olives, pickles)

Directions:

Mix the fruits into the cheese and spread between the cakes OR send the fruits along in their own container to be sprinkled on, as the child desires.

Build a Nacho

Don't assume that all pre-packaged foods aren't healthy. Just look at the range of whole foods and organic foods that can be bought in jars in supermarkets or homemade local markets. Salsa is a great example. Keep your own shredded cheese mixes in the freezer for quick uses.

Ingredients:

15-20 tortilla chips (low salt ones are healthier, so are blue and flaxseed options)

1/3 cup salsa

1/3 cup shredded cheese

¼ shredded cooked chicken

1 tbsp sliced green onion (optional)

1 tbsp sliced olives (optional)

Directions:

Pack it all up in separate containers. Little fingers love to make little meals. Let each chip get its own treatment. Send along a wet wipe.

Rollin' Rollin' Rollin'

With a little imagination, and the right ingredients on hand, rollup portable food is pretty easy. Stock up on: cold cuts, the leaner the better, cream cheese, thinly sliced cheese, and assorted thinly stripped vegetables.

Here are some great combinations:

Ingredients:

Ham, Swiss with a creamy dressing and asparagus

Turkey, Havarti and melon slivers

Ham, cheddar and apple slivers

Roast beef, cream cheese and pepper slivers

Kielbassa loaf with cream cheese and jalapeno jelly

Cold Chicken Noodle Salad

Cold chicken is one of the easiest leftovers to keep on hand, and even more accessible with store-bought rotisserie chicken always ready in the store. Load it up with some crunchy vegetable and slurpy noodles and kids of all ages will dig in.

Ingredients:

4 oz. cooked noodle – whole wheat pasta work well, or quick cooking rice noodles

4 oz cooked shredded chicken

1 shredded carrot

1 red bell pepper in strips

1 sliced stalk of celery

½ cup sliced snow peas

¼ cup sliced green onions

¼ cup bottled sesame ginger salad dressing

Directions:

Combine and store tightly in container. Make 2-3 servings.

Panzanella

You may find requests for this again and again. And it's such a great way to use of day old bread. If bread is too "fresh", toast it a little. Too soft will make the dressing sog it all up.

Ingredients:

1 cup chunky cubes of Italian bread, with crusts

½ cup firm chunks tomato (leave juice and seeds on the cutting board)

¼ cup slivered Parmesan cheese (take a potato peeler to a block)

¼ cup diced red pepper/green pepper mix

¼ cup celery

¼ cup cubed or sliced Italian cold cuts (salami, prosciutto, mortadella)

Basil, salt, pepper to taste

2 tbsp Italian salad dressing

Directions:

Mix together everything and drizzle with the dressing. The bread will absorb much of it, but firm bread should hold up until lunchtime.

Greek Twist – use feta cheese, olives, cucumbers and pieces of cold pork, chicken or lamb instead of the cold cuts. Use red wine vinegar, olive oil, lemon juice, and oregano for a dressing. Toss in a few mint leaves and it's really authentic! Opa!

Granola Parfait

One of the trendiest ideas in portable food has become the Mason Jar meal. These are excellent food containers with nice secure lids that can be reused again and again. The caution however, especially with children, is that they are glass. If you can use a plastic version for your child you may prevent a lunch box disaster.

Ingredients:

4 oz yogurt any style, any flavor

4 oz granola – any flavor

4 oz fresh fruit – berries, apple, pear, peach, citrus

Directions:

Start with a layer of 2 tbsps granola in bottom of container. Add 2 tbsps of yogurt, then 2 tbsps of fruit of choice. Repeat layer to top of the container. Really great for eating with a long spoon, even in the car seat! (Save those long plastic sundae spoons from the ice cream shops).

Salad in a Jar

Packing a salad, or whole meal in a jar is a great idea, especially if the jar will not get tipped over or be in an environment where it can be broken. Start with the dressing in the bottom, the heaviest vegetables on top, and work your way to the lighter items like meats, cheese and finally the greens. Turn it out into a bowl at lunch time, or jab it with a fork and stir up what you can. An upside down shake or two can move around a thinner dressing too.

Ingredients:

2 oz of dressing – avoid creamy ones unless being tossed into a bowl

2-3 oz of hard vegetables/fruits – carrots, celery, apples, peppers, onions

2-3 oz softer choices – tomatoes, onion, beans, pasta, rice,

2 oz – cheese and proteins

Directions:

Fill the jar to overflowing with green and press the lid down to compact it. That will keep ingredients from shifting.

Roast Beef Pita Pockets

Pita bread is one of the most versatile. It doesn't get squashed up because it is already so flat. The key to a great pita pocket is to cut it so the flap tucks back in when it's stuffed.

Ingredients:

Per pocket –

2 tbsps cream cheese, mayonnaise or Caesar salad dressing

3-4 slices thinly sliced roast beef

1 slice swiss cheese

2 tbsp alfalfa sprouts

Directions:

Cut open a pita pocket. Spread the inside of the pocket with the cheese. Fill with beef and cheese and top with sprouts. Tuck flap of the pocket back in over the sprouts.

Soft Chicken Tacos

With all the ingredients handy, do-it-yourself tacos are a cinch!

Ingredients:

2 tbsps mashed avocado in an airtight container, sprinkled with lemon juice

2 oz shredded cooked chicken

2 oz shredded lettuce (add a sliced green onion to it!)

2 oz shredded Monterey Jack cheese

2 soft whole wheat tortillas

2 oz salsa in a separate container

Directions:

Assemble in whatever order is desired!

Make Ahead

Big batches to last all week

Families with many children have always known the benefits of planning ahead. Not only is it economical to feed a large family by preparing batches in large quantities, making up large quantities of favorite dishes on the weekend or early in the week frees up the need to think each day about what to pack for lunch. Choose a lunch of the week and make it work for every day. Or make up two and alternate for variety.

Cold dishes to make up early and keep in the fridge

Sundried Tomato Pasta

Pasta salads can be great without mayonnaise type dressings. This is a great energy-booster for kids and keeps all week in the fridge because it doesn't involve lettuce, just hard crunchy vegetables.

Ingredients:

2 cups cooked whole wheat macaroni

½ cup diced red and green pepper

½ cup diced celery

¼ cup diced red onion

1 cup cooked chicken shredded or cubed

1 cup cooked but tender-crisp, broccoli

4-6 small bocconcini (mini mozzarella balls) diced

1/3 cup bottled sundried tomato dressing

pepper to taste

squeeze of lemon juice

Directions:

Cook pasta and rinse. Cook broccoli and rinse. Toss all tog
ether with dressing.

Keep covered and refrigerated up to a week.

Glassy Shrimp Noodle Salad

This is such a favorite that it often makes an appearance at Potluck dinners.

Ingredients:

½ package of vermicelli or spaghetti.

20-24 medium cooked shrimp

3 large grated carrots

2 stalks celery slivered

3 sliced green onions

Dressing:

1/3 cup soya sauce

¼ cup white vinegar

2 tsps thai chili sauce * adjust to taste

2 tsps sugar

1" chunk fresh ginger peeled and chopped

4 garlic cloves, minced

2 tsp. chili flakes

1/4 cup canola oil

Directions:

Cook and cool noodles. Toss shrimp with vegetables and add dressing. Pour all of it over the noodles and toss thoroughly.

Chinese Rice Salad

The raisins in this give the overall Asian flavors a tad of sweet. And the rice has such flavor the longer it sits in the fridge…if it last all week!

Ingredients:

Sauce – 1 hour before serving

¼ cup soya sauce

½ cup oil (peanut, or canola)

1 tsp vinegar (rice wine is best)

1 minced clove garlic

Pepper

1 tsp lemon juice

Salad –

3 cups cooked rice (Minute rice is fine!)

½ cup cashews (optional for nut free environments)

2 cups slivered Romaine lettuce (or mix with spinach)

½ green pepper diced

½ cup sliced mushrooms

2-3 cups bean sprouts

¼ cup raisins

½ cup celery, diced

3 green onions diced

Chunky Chicken Salad

Enjoy this in so many ways... wrapped in lettuce leaves, stuffed in a pita or wrapped in a tortilla. Skip the grapes and it works well as a sandwich filling, especially in a crusty bun.

Ingredients:

2 cups cooked cubed chicken (or turkey leftovers)

½ cup diced celery

¼ cup diced red or green peppers

¼ cup diced onions (red or green)

2 tbsps chopped fresh basil

3-4 tbsps mayonnaise

½ cup grapes, sliced in half

¼ cup cashews or almonds * optional for nut free environment

salt and pepper to taste

Directions:

Mix all together and store in airtight container up to a week in fridge.

Cook these up early in the week and reheat or serve cold each day.

Pizza Muffins

There are lots of ways to eat pizza, but not all ways get the gooeyness of the cheese to make each bite delectable. Even at room temperature, these nuggets re-invent pizza on a whole new level.

Ingredients:

1 cup white flour

1 cup whole wheat flour

1 tbsp sugar

1 tbsp baking powder

1 tsp basil

1 tsp salt

1 cup small cubes of sharp cheddar cheese

1 cup plain yogurt

2 eggs

¼ cup melted butter

½ cup diced red and green peppers

¼ cup marinara sauce

½ cup shredded mozzarella

Directions:

Preheat oven to 400°F. Line 12 muffin cups with paper liners. In a large bowl, whisk together dry ingredients. Stir in cheddar cubes. In another bowl, whisk together eggs, yogurt and butter until smooth. . Stir into flour until combined and stir in peppers. Batter will be very thick. Spoon into muffin tins evenly. Top each with 1 tsp of sauce then cheese.

Bake 20 minutes until golden, let cool and store in airtight container.

Potato Pockets

Ingredients:

3 medium sized potatoes , diced (peeling is optional)

2 tbsps canola oil

1 small diced onion

1 clove minced garlic

1 cup sausage meat (squeeze meat out of casings or use bulk meat)

½ tsp salt

½ tsp dried thyme

1 sheet frozen puff pastry, thawed

1 large egg slightly beaten

flour for dusting

Directions:

Preheat oven to 425°F.

Heat oil and cook potatoes over medium heat about 10 minutes, turning and browning. Stir in onion, garlic and sausage, breaking up the meat to incorporate a hash. Cook about 3-4 minutes until meat is cooked. Stir in salt and thyme and cool. Divide in to four portions.

On a wooden surface, dust with flour and unroll pastry into a 12" square. Cut into quarters of 6" squares. Place a portion of sausage mixture on each quarter. Gently fold one corner over mixture and seal into a triangle. Brush with egg as a "glue" and across the top.

Bake on a baking sheet covered with parchment for 20 minutes. Great cold , or warmed up in a microwave.

Coconut Shrimp

Stock up when shrimp go on sale. These are great for pairing with veggies and dip for a fast "finger food" lunch on the go.

Ingredients:

20-24 raw medium shrimp

½ cup shredded coconut

1 envelope chicken coating mix

canola oil cooking spray

Directions:

Preheat oven to 425°F . Line a baking sheet with parchment. Toss shrimp in a bowl and spray with oil. In another bowl, mix coating mix and coconut. Toss over the shrimp to evenly coat. Lay shrimp in sheet and bake 12-15 minutes until coconut is toasted and shrimp are firm.

Zippy Chicken Tenders

Kids love chicken nuggets...but parents hate the quality of the chicken, the additives and the fat and sodium content. Start offering up these alternatives and nuggets will be a thing of the past.

Ingredients:

12-15 chicken strips (1" wide strips of breast meat, or tenders)

2 eggs

2 tbsps mayonnaise

1/2 cup panko crumbs

¼ cup Parmesan cheese

½ tsp sea salt

½ tsp steak spice or pepper mix

Directions:

Preheat oven to 450°F. Line a baking sheet with non stick foil or parchment. Lay strips out on paper towel to dry them thoroughly. In separate bowl, whisk eggs and stir in the mayo. In another bowl, mix crumbs, cheese and seasonings.

Dip each strip in wet mixture, then dry, to thoroughly coat. Lay each strip on sheet and bake 12-15 minutes until crisp and firm. Cool and store airtight.

Grizadilla

Stock up on smoked gouda when it goes on sale because it is the special flavor that makes these a favorite, hot or cold.

Ingredients:

4 whole wheat tortillas

2 medium onions

2 tbsps butter or margarine

1 tbsp canola oil

1 tbsp sugar

4 tbsps bottled barbeque sauce, any brand

2 cups shredded cooked chicken (or leftover turkey)

2 cups shredded smoked gouda cheese (Monterey Jack is a reasonable substitute)

Directions:

In a medium skillet, heat butter and oil. Add in thinly sliced onion and sauté slowly, stirring often. When glassy, sprinkle with sugar and continue to caramelize. Remove from heat when done.

Preheat oven to 425 °F. On two baking sheets, lay out the four tortillas. Spread a tablespoon of barbeque sauce over each. Spread onions evenly over all four. Toss chicken on top of each and then cheese.

Bake five minutes, then remove, fold oven to quesadilla shape and continue baking 3-4 more minutes until edges crisp. Remove from oven and serve hot or let cool for lunches. Great hot or cold.

Pizza Pinwheels

Don't wait until your kids are in college to discover they enjoy cold pizza. These are great out of the oven or room temperature n the lunch box. If they like their pizza a little saucier, send along a little dipping container of Marinara Sauce.

Ingredients:

2 cups self-raising flour

pinch of salt

½ cup butter, cut into cubes

2/3 cup milk

3 tbsps tomato paste

1 tsp basil

1 tsp garlic salt

pepper

1 cups shredded mozzarella cheese (or a store bought pizza mix)

12-16 slices of pepperoni chopped up into smaller bits

1 egg slightly beaten

flour for dusting

Directions:

Preheat oven to 400°F. Line a baking sheet with parchment paper. Sift together salt and flour and cut into the butter until it resembles bread crumbs. Stir in milk and form a dough. Turn the dough onto a floured surface and gently knead about 3 minutes. Add more flour if it is too sticky. Roll out into a 12" x 24" rectangle. Spread with the paste, seasonings, and pepperoni, then the cheese. Turn the dough so the long end is in front of you and roll up. Slice into 10-12 pieces and place side –by –side on the sheet. Touching is okay as it helps with the rising. Brush with the beaten egg.

Bake 25 minutes, and cool.

Crescent Surprises

Store bought crescent rolls make great one-hander easy lunch items. Even a day or two after they have been in the fridge, the dough stands up to cold, at room temperature, or warmed up quickly in a microwave.

Directions:

Bake about two minutes longer than the package instructions.

Work on a floured surface, separate the crescents and try these combinations:

Cheddar and Ham - Sprinkle shredded cheddar and cubes of ham over each crescent. Add a few dabs of honey mustard and roll them up.

Pig in a Blanket – Use a breakfast sausage or hotdog for this old classic. Add cheese of any type to really step it up.

Vegetarian Roll – spread cream cheese, 2-4 pepper strips, a sliced mushroom and 1 tsp. of sundried tomatoes to each and roll it up.

Hot Choices

For thermal bottles & microwaves

Soups, stews and casseroles are the perfect make-ahead meal and are real budget stretchers. Invest in good wide mouth thermal bottles to make these belly warmers portable, and much appreciated when a hot lunch hits the spot. There really isn't a soup, stew or casserole that doesn't freeze well, even when portioned in small containers to be re-heated where a microwave oven is available.

Loaded Potato Soup

If you love a loaded baked potato, you'll enjoy all the same all the components in a soup. This is particularly handy if you have leftover baked or roasted potatoes you want to use up.

Ingredients:

2 -3 large baking potatoes (or cubed cooked leftovers, about 3 cups)

1 can chicken broth or stock

1 cup milk

½ tsp thyme

salt and pepper to taste

Toppings:

3-4 slices bacon

3 green onions

1 cup cheddar cheese

1 cup broccoli florets (optional)

sour cream for garnish

Directions:

Microwave potatoes for 5 minutes, turn over and microwave for another 5 minutes.

In a pot, slightly crush potatoes with a masher. (Leave some chunks if you like.) Add the broth, milk and seasonings, and simmer for 20 minutes. Meanwhile cook bacon, drain on paper towels and crumble. Cook broccoli to desired tenderness. Slice onions.

To serve in thermal bottles, add toppings of choice before closing the lid, making sure sour cream is last.

French Canadian Pea

A ham bone is usually only available to you after the holidays, or if you know a good butcher. But a good substitute is to use a 2 lb. piece of peameal back bacon. The peameal can be strained out of the stock before the rest of the ingredients are added.

Ingredients:

6 quarts water

1 ham bone

3 bay leaves

2-3 sprigs fresh thyme

1 quartered onion (keep core on)

1-2 carrots, in big chunks

¼ cup chopped celery tops

Directions:

Add all this to the pot of water and simmer 2-3 hours. Strain.

Add 2 cups dried split yellow peas. Cook another 1-2 hours.

Half hour before serving add 1 finely diced onion, 1 tiny diced small carrot and 1 rib of tiny diced celery. Add ham from the bone, or the back bacon crumbled, if you like a meaty soup.

White Soup

It's funny to hear nutritionists talk about avoiding "white foods" like white bread, sugar, flour...but there sure are a lot of healthy white choices that make this soup a family favorite.

Ingredients:

4 cups chicken or turkey, broth or stock

2 cups cauliflower florets

1 diced onion

2 cups peeled and diced white potatoes

1 cup diced celery (aim for the "white" ends if you want to keep the soup white)

1 cup diced white mushrooms

2 whole heads of roasted garlic, squeezed out

1 cup milk

2 cups shredded or diced cooked chicken or turkey (optional for vegetarians)

salt, pepper to taste (white pepper if you have it)

Directions:

Cook vegetables in broth or stock until tender. Scoop out half and puree in blender or food processor, then return to the pot so it is a mix of smooth and chunky. Add milk, meat and season with salt and pepper. Simmer.

Beef Barley Soup

Barley just isn't as common a grain as it was in our parent's, and grandparent's day. But it's a great addition to soups for its heaviness and nutty flavor. Kids like it. This soup is perfect for leftover roast beef or cheaper cuts of beef, especially when they go on sale.

Ingredients:

1 pound of beef top round steak, cut into small cubes (2 cups leftover roast beef)

1 tbsp canola oil (not needed if beef is cooked)

3 cans (14 oz each) beef broth (look for low sodium!)

2 cups water

1/3 cup pearl barley

salt and pepper to taste

1 cup peas, fresh or frozen

1 cup chopped carrots

¾ cup chopped celery

½ cup chopped onion

3 tbsp minced fresh parsley

Directions:

In a large stockpot, heat oil and stir fry steak for 2 minutes. Add broth, water, barley and seasonings. Simmer for 2 hours, stirring occasionally. Add vegetables, more water or stock if a thinner consistency is desired.

Chunky Chicken Soup

Chicken soup is a standard, especially when you are feeling poorly. But make it heavier and it eats more like a meal when loaded with lots of harvest goodness.

Ingredients:

Bones from one rotisserie chicken

4 cups water

1 onion – quartered with core on

1 stalk celery (or use the ends you might normally discard)

½ cup chopped celery leaves

2 carrots in cubes

2-3 sprigs thyme (or 2 tbsps dried)

3-4 leaves of sage (or 1 tbsp dried)

1 tsp salt

½ tsp pepper

Directions:

Preheat oven to 400°F. On a baking sheet covered with non-stick foil, lay the bones. Roast for 30 minutes. This makes a HUGE difference in the flavor of the stock.

In a big stockpot, add bones, to water, with all the rest. Simmer 2-3 hours.

Strain.

Return to the pot.

2-3 cups of chicken or turkey chunks (about what the rotisserie chicken yields)

1 cup chunky celery

1 cup chunky carrots

1 cup diced onion

1 cup peas

1 cup diced mushrooms

1 cup green and red pepper (optional)

1 cup milk

1 cup cooked rotini pasta (optional)

season to taste with salt, pepper, thyme, garlic powder, sage

Thai Spaghetti

There is no substitute for the creamy texture and flavor of a great peanut sauce in a Thai dish, but if nut products are restricted in your child's environment, save this one for another place, or enjoy it at home.

Ingredients:

2 tbsp coconut oil

1 thinly sliced carrot

2 ribs celery sliced

1 large onion sliced in slivers

½ cup snow peas sliced in half

2 tbsps minced ginger

2 tbsp mince garlic

2 cups cooked chicken

1 cup peanut sauce

½ pkg spaghetti or linguini

lime juice

2 tbsps chopped cilantro

2 tbsps chopped peanuts

Directions:

Cook pasta, drain but save the pasta water. In a wok, heat oil and start stir-frying vegetable in order, about a minute between each. Add chicken and sauce and simmer. Add pasta and toss, using a little pasta water to get the sauce to a consistency you like. Serve with a squeeze of lime, toss on some cilantro and peanuts.

Jambalaya

A great one pot dinner that makes great leftovers, or just make up a double batch so there are sure to be lunch portions. Frozen shrimp and Oktoberfest sausages are easy to keep on hand in the freezer and whenever there is leftover cooked chicken around get started. When chicken thighs go on sale, stock up because they are so flavorful in this dish.

Ingredients:

3 strips bacon

2 Oktoberfest sausage (or any other type)

½ red pepper diced

½ green pepper diced

1 large rib of celery diced

1 medium onion diced

2 cloves garlic minced

16-18 raw shrimp

2 cooked chicken thighs (or leftovers from a rotisserie chicken)

1 tomato diced

2 tbsps Worcestershire sauce

3 bay leaves

1 tbsp bay seasoning

½ tsp celery salt

1 tbsp hot sauce (or to taste)

1/2 tsp Tabasco sauce (or to taste)

1 cup clamato juice

2 cups cooked brown rice, or one packet of Bistro brown rice ready to serve.

Directions:

Cook the bacon in a large skillet or walk. Remove when crispy to paper towels. Into the fat, toss sliced sausage, and cook until sausage is brown. Add in peppers and celery, onions and garlic and continue sautéing. Add shrimp, and cook until they are pink. Add everything else in order. Simmer.

Manicotti

Making up batches of these and freezing them, make them so easy to portion for every sized appetite in your family. They can even be portioned individually. All the flavor of lasagna, but easier to manage and serve. If your thermal bottle is round, just cut the manicotti in half, or chop it for smaller eaters.

Ingredients:

1 box of manicotti - usually contain 14

1 pound of ground beef (half in ground pork or sausage is good!)

1 clove garlic chopped

1 tbsp parsley

1 tbsp basil

1 ½ tsp.salt

1 can, about 2 cups , tomatoes diced or rough chopped

13 oz can of tomato paste

3 cups medium curd cottage cheese

2 beaten eggs

1 tsp salt

½ tsp pepper

2 tbsp fresh chopped parsley

½ cup grated Parmesan cheese

1 cup shredded mozzarella cheese

Directions:

Cook the pasta to al dente, drain and cool. Brown and drain the beef, stir in garlic, seasonings, tomatoes and paste. Simmer. In a separate bowl, whisk eggs and add cottage cheese, seasoning and Parmesan.

To assemble: lay baking dish with 1 cup of meat tomato mixture. Using a teaspoon, carefully stuff each manicotti shell with cheese filling. Lay stuffed pasta on tomato mixture. Top all the stuffed with rest of tomato meat mixture and top with mozzarella. Bake for 30 minutes, or refrigerate in singles or pairs for individual lunches.

Tuna Surprise

This may be a throwback to the 60's but is still a favorite for the lunchbox. Fans of cold pasta dishes will enjoy it right out of the container, but heated up make it creamy with the crunchy topping being the "surprise'!

Ingredients:

2 cans drained tuna

2 cups cooked egg noodles

1 can mushroom soup

1 tbsp butter

½ cup diced celery

½ cup diced onion

1 cup diced mushrooms

2 cloves minced garlic

½ cup milk

salt, pepper to taste

¼ cup Parmesan cheese

¼ cup bread crumbs

½ cup French fried onion toppers

cooking spray

Directions:

Preheat oven to 400°F. Cook and drain pasta. In a large microwaveable bowl, melt butter in microwave. Add celery and cook for 1 minute. Add onion and cook again for another minute. Stir in the rest of the vegetables. Stir in the tuna, breaking it up as you work. Add in condensed soup and milk, then cold noodles and seasonings. Pour into a heavy casserole dish that was spray with cooking spray. Sprinkle remaining items over top and spray to moisten. Bake 40 mins. Serve up in lunch containers.

Best Ever Shepherd's Pie

This will become your family's favorite leftover...if there are any portions left after dinner.

Ingredients:

1 lb minced beef

½ lb minced pork (4-5 sausages out of their casing works well)

1 medium carrot diced tiny

1 rib celery diced tiny

½ cup red and green peppers diced small

3 cloves minced garlic

1 onion

2 tbsp beef gravy mix

¼ cup water

1 tbsp Worcestershire sauce

salt and pepper

½ cup peas

1 cup shredded cheese mix (cheddar, mozzarella, is good)

1 package frozen tater tots (or 2 cups half cooked hash browns as a substitute)

Directions:

Preheat oven to 425°F. Brown the meats in a large skillet breaking them up well. Drain most of it but leave about a tablespoon of fat in the pan. Remove the meat and sauté the carrots and celery in the remaining fat. After a minute, add the onion and garlic. Add meat to the vegetables and then the gravy mix, water and seasonings. Stir in the peas. Pour this into a shallow casserole dish sprayed with cooking spray. Sprinkle with the cheese. Top with one layer of the tater tots. Bake 20 minutes until tater tots are crispy.

Breakfast

On the go goodness

For years, nutritionists have been promoting eating healthy foods for breakfast, to break us all of the habits of choosing heavy carbs, sweet laced pastries and greasy meats. The trick is to make breakfast easy so it doesn't get skipped, or made up of processed items that are too easily available.

Egg Cups

Eggs are a great breakfast food, but can't always be eaten at the table with a knife and fork. Find your child's favorite additions and make up batches for the freezer or fridge.

Ingredients:

¼ cup milk or cream

3 eggs

1/3 cup Parmesan cheese

¼ cup diced cooked ham

¼ cup frozen corn

1 tbsp green onion

salt, pepper to taste

paprika to garnish

Directions:

Preheat oven to 375°F. Line muffin pan with paper wrappers. Whisk the eggs and add the milk. Stir in all the rest but sprinkle top with paprika. Spoon half way into cups and bake 20 minutes until lightly golden. Cool completely. Store in an airtight container.

French Toast Fingers

Avoiding the sticky syrup that ends up everywhere when kids eat...especially in the car, is achieved with these. The bit of sweet is grilled in and you can control how much sweet you want to offer up early in the morning!

Ingredients:

2 eggs

¼ cup milk

2 tsps sugar

½ tsp vanilla

8 slices whole wheat sandwich bread

favourite half-sugar jam or jelly

Directions:

Heat up a large skillet with non-stick spray. Whisk together eggs, milk, sugar, vanilla and set aside. Make "sandwiches" out of the bread and jam, (trim crusts only if your kids insist on it) Cut each sandwich into three "sticks". Dip each stick into the egg mixture and grill until

85

golden on each side. On busy mornings, just pop a few in the microwave for a warmup and enjoy on the go.

Oatmeal To Go Cakes

Preheat oven to 350°F. Line a baking sheet with parchment paper.

Ingredients:

½ cup butter or soy margarine

½ cup shortening

¼ cup brown sugar

¼ cup white sugar

3 tbsps boiling water

½ tsp baking soda

¼ tsp salt

½ tsp cinnamon

¾ cup white flour (or add in some parts coconut flour and almond flour)

¾ cup whole wheat flour

1 ½ cup rolled oats, pulsed to a flour in a food processor

½ cup raisins (optional)

Directions:

Cream the butter, shortening and sugars with a mixer. Mix the water with the soda, then add it in too. Add in the dry ingredients and mix thoroughly. Roll out on a floured surface to desired thickness. Cut into bars, or into shapes using cookie cutters. Place on sheet and bake 7-8 minutes, or more for a crispier bar.

Breakfast Corn Dogs

Who doesn't love a corn dog? This version takes its inspiration from the McDonald's McGriddle Sandwich. So expect some essence of maple syrup in the batter to make for a more succulent taste to the traditional corn dog. And swap out the frankfurter for a breakfast link...so yummy!

Ingredients:

14 Candy apple sticks (found at bulk or craft stores)

14 breakfast sausage links

2 quarts vegetable oil for deep frying

1 cup medium grind cornmeal

1 cup flour

1 cup milk

½ tsp salt

2 large eggs

2 tbsp maple syrup

2 tbsps sugar

Directions:

Preheat oven to 250°F. Line a baking sheet with parchment paper. .

Cook the sausage in a skillet and drain on paper toweling. Heat the pil to deep fry temperature of 360°F.

Insert a candy stick in each sausage, ensuring a portion of the stick is exposed for handling. Whisk the eggs, milk, syrup, and sugar together. Add the cornmeal and flour until a smooth batter forms. Pour the batter into a tall narrow glass for dipping the sausages. Rotate the sausage around so it is evenly coated, then place carefully into the hot oil. Turn occasionally and cook about 3 minutes until golden brown. Remove from oil and lay on wire rack over a baking sheet. Keep warm in a low oven while the other corn dogs are being fried. About 4 at a time works well. Serve with extra syrup for dipping or cool and freeze for later. Can be reheated in a 350°F oven for 15 mins.

Egg Paninis

It's amazing how much toasting a sandwich can enhance the taste. And little ones don't mind a cold version of a grilled sandwich. A great tip for a better grilling surface is to slice a little off the top and bottom of a bun to expose the inside bread. It will crisp up better with some spray or butter on it.

Ingredients:

8 large eggs

2 tbsps icy cold water

salt and pepper

8 thinly sliced deli meat – smoked turkey or prosciutto work well

2 tbsps butter

8 slices cheese, Swiss or sharp cheddar work well.

4 soft rolls, halved lengthwise

Directions:

Whisk the eggs together, and trickle in the water, then the salt and pepper. In a large skillet , melt the butters and pour in the egg mixture, and cook to a scramble. Divide the egg mixture among the four buns. Top each with cheese and meat. Clean the egg pan and use another with cooking spray of butter to grill the sandwiches until crispy and cheese is melted through. A panini press works well too.

Mega Muffins

It can be tricky to suggest a muffin for breakfast because it sounds like dessert, but if you pack it with a load of healthy ingredients, it can go over well. Preheat oven to 375°F. Line muffin tin with paper liners.

Ingredients:

1 cup whole wheat flour

1 cup made up of almond flour, oat flour, and coconut flour* (use all whole wheat if muffins are going to a nut free environment)

½ cup white sugar

½ cup brown sugar

2 tsp baking soda

2 tsps ground cinnamon

1 tsp ground ginger

2 cups shredded carrots

1/3 cup chopped dried apricot

1/3 cup sunflower seeds

1/3 cup flaked or shredded coconut

1/3 cup raisins

1/3 cup dried cranberries

1 medium mashed ripe banana

3 eggs

1 cup canola oil

2 tsp vanilla extract

Directions:

Mix together dry ingredients. In a separate bowl, mix together carrots and all the fruits. In another bowl, beat eggs, add in oil and vanilla then stir in the carrot mixture. Stir in the dry ingredients and when mixed well, spoon into 12 muffins for large, or 18 for medium. Cool for 5 minutes. They freeze really well!

Apple Breakfast Bars

These are great for on the go, and can even double for snacks. To change them up , substitute apple filling with berry mixtures or low sugar pie fillings.

Ingredients:

3 apples, peeled, cored and thinly sliced

1 tbsp brown sugar

1 tbsp butter

pinch of sea salt

1 cup whole wheat flour

1 cup ground oatmeal

¼ cup packed brown sugar

1 tbsp flax seed

½ cup melted butter

Directions:

Preheat oven to 350°F. Line an 8" square pan with parchment. Melt butter in a medium skillet, add apples, sugar and salt, and cook 5-7 minutes on a simmer. Remove the chunky mixture and let cool slightly.

Meanwhile mix dry ingredients and pour in melted butter, mix until crumbs form. Pat half into the pan. Spread with filling and crumb the other half and gently press the top layer into the filling.

Bake 45 minutes until golden and top looks cracked. Let cool completely, then cut into bars.

Devilled Eggs

Some kids will eat these anytime…breakfast, snacks, parties. Very easy to keep on hand in the fridge, or to pack tightly in a container.

Ingredients:

6 eggs hard cooked and peeled

2 green onions very finely chopped

2 tbsps mayonnaise

2 tbsps seafood sauce (or a mixture of horseradish and ketchup, squirt of lemon)

salt and pepper to taste

paprika to garnish

Directions:

Peel eggs and slice very carefully longwise. Pop out yolk and mix it with all remaining ingredients except paprika. Refill each half egg white with the filling and sprinkle with paprika.

Bacon and Cheddar Waffles

Don't think of waffles as just a Sunday Brunch option. When cooked to crispy they can work well for small sandwiches that don't get soggy like some breads. Lots of things can be added to the batter for variety. This is a great one that only requires a smidge of syrup for dipping.

Ingredients:

6 slices cooked drained and roughly chopped bacon

1 cup flour

¾ cup of mixed coconut, almond and whole wheat flour

2 tbsps sugar

2 tsp baking powder

1 ½ tsp salt

2 eggs, separated

3 tbsps canola oil

1 ¾ cup milk (some of this could be almond milk)

2 cups grated sharp cheddar

Maple syrup for dipping

Directions:

Preheat waffle iron.

Whisk dry ingredients together and set aside. In a separate bowl, whisk egg yolks, milk and oil together., add in the dry ingredients, then the cheese and bacon, but don't over mix. Separately whip egg whites and fold into the batter. Spoon batter onto waffle iron and cook until desired crispness. Serve with maple syrup.

Waffle sandwiches – spread cream cheese or cinnamon spread between two for a great breakfast.

Sausage Balls

These are great as a snack, with veggies or soup for a meal, or a breakfast on the go. They make a great appetizer to for a party or to bring to a potluck because they are just as great at room temperature.

Ingredients:

½ lb sausage meet (half a tube)

1 ¼ cup biscuit mix

1 ½ cup shredded sharp cheddar

2 green onions minced

salt and pepper

2 tbsps cream

Directions:

Preheat oven to 350°F. Line a baking sheet with parchment or non stick foil. Mix together and form into 1 inch balls. Brush with cream and bake 18-20 mins. Turn once half way through. Serve warm , or reheat later, or wrap in foil for a room temperature lunch box item. Makes about 24.

Granola Cones

This is great for kids to munch on, a cereal that doesn't need milk. Make paper cones out of newspaper or cardboard, then line with another paper cone of waxed paper. Fun to eat, and easy for car trips.

Ingredients:

5 cups (1.25 L) wheat-free rolled oats

½ cup (125 mL) chopped walnuts* (optional, or substitute with more dried fruits)

½ cup (125 mL) chopped whole almonds*

1/3 cup (75 mL) raw sunflower seeds

1/3 cup (75 mL) raw pumpkin seeds

1/3 cup (75 mL) dried cranberries

1/3 cup (75 mL) sliced dried apricots

¼ cup (60 mL) sultana raisins

¼ cup (60 mL) packed brown sugar

2 tbsp (30 mL) flaxseeds

2 tbsp (30 mL) sesame seeds

1/3 cup (75 mL) brown rice syrup

¼ cup (60 mL) liquid honey

¼ cup (60 mL) canola oil or butter, melted

½ tsp (2 mL) cinnamon

½ tsp (2 mL) salt

Directions:

In large bowl, combine oats, hazelnuts, almonds, sunflower seeds, pumpkin seeds, cranberries, apricots, raisins, brown sugar, flaxseeds and sesame seeds.

In saucepan, heat together rice syrup, honey, oil, cinnamon and salt over medium heat until blended, about 3 minutes. Pour over oat mixture; toss to coat.

Spread evenly on 2 greased or parchment paper–lined rimmed baking sheets. Bake in 325°F oven, stirring every 10 minutes and rotating pans halfway through, until golden, about 25 minutes. Let cool. Store in airtight container for up to 3 weeks.

Pack a Punch Breakfast Bars

Discover just how much goodness can be packed into this flavourful bar. Wrap them individually or keep them in an airtight container for everyone to enjoy.

(great to stash a few in the glove compartment...but don't forget about them)

Ingredients:

1 cup whole wheat flour

1/4 cup white flour

1/4 cup coconut flour

3/4 cup brown sugar

½ tsp baking soda

½ tsp baking powder

½ tsp each cinnamon, nutmeg, salt

¼ tsp each nutmeg, cloves

3 tbsp ground flax seed

3 tbsps wheat germ

3 tbsp ground almonds

1/3 cup applesauce

3 tbsp canola oil

3 tbsp milk

2 eggs, whisked

¾ tsp vanilla

¼ cup honey

1 small apple, peeled, cored, chopped fine

½ cup walnuts *optional

½ cup raisins, or pistachios, or dried cranberries or dried apricots * optional

Directions:

Preheat oven to 350°F. Grease or line with parchment a 8x12" baking sheet. In a large bowl, mix all dry ingredients together. In a separate bowl , mix all the wet listed until the honey. Slowly start adding the wet to the dry, then stir in the rest and use your hands if it's easier. Pour mixture onto tray and pat down. Dust your fingers with flour if it is too sticky. Bake 8-10 minutes and then cool thoroughly before cutting into bars.

Squash, Carrot, Raisin Bread

A hearty bread chock full of goodness can be a great breakfast food. Spread with a little cream cheese, or a favorite nut spread and you've a protein packed breakfast that's easy to eat...wherever you are headed.

Ingredients:

7/8 cup white flour

¾ cup whole wheat flour

1 tsp cinnamon

¼ tsp nutmeg

pinch of ground ginger

½ tsp salt

1 tsp baking soda

¾ stick softened butter

1/2 cup honey

1 tsp vanilla

1/3 cup vegetable oil

2 eggs

½ cup finely grated summer squash or zucchini

¼ cup finely grated carrots

1/3 cup sunflower seeds

½ cup raisins

Directions:

Preheat oven to 325°F. Line a loaf pan with parchment paper. Grease 9x9 square pan. Grate vegetables, and mix together dry ingredients. In food processor or mixer, cream butter and honey together, add oil, eggs and vanilla. Stir in raisins. Stir wet ingredients into dry and fold in vegetables, seeds and raisins. Pour into pan and bake 35 -40 mins. Cool thoroughly before slicing.

More
Veggies
Please!

Variety is the key

There have been a lot of trends in family recipes to disguise vegetables…puree them into brownies and cakes, or sneak them into ravioli or soups and stews. True, many vegetables work well as fillings and additions to many dishes, but children need to learn to eat vegetables in their honest states too! Variety is the key here…surprise yourself with what kids will try!

No Fry Potato Skins.

Super tasty, super healthy.

Ingredients:

4 large russet potatoes

vegetable oil

½ cup shredded sharp cheddar

2 green onions slices

2 strips cooked crispy bacon, cut in to bits

cayenne pepper

sour cream for garnish

Directions:

Bake the potatoes in the oven or a microwave. (This is great for leftover potatoes) When they are done, cut them long ways into two boats. Hollow them out to about ¼ inch of the skin. Use your fingers to coat these boats in the oil and lay bottom up on a tin foil lined cookie sheet. Roast for 10 minutes, then turn them over and cook another 5 minutes. Mix the cheese, onions and bacon and sprinkle it evenly over the 8 halves. Sprinkle a little cayenne pepper on each and return to the oven for a few minutes until cheese melts and edges brown. Top with sour cream.

Mango and Black Bean Salad

This keeps so well in the fridge for a few days. Great for potlucks, or add some protein like chicken or shrimp for a whole meal.

Ingredients:

½ can well drained and rinsed black beans (the other half freezes well)

1 diced mango

1 cup diced red and green pepper

1 rib celery diced

½ cup diced red onion

2 tbsp olive oil

1 tbsp balsamic vinegar

squeeze of lemon juice

salt and pepper to taste

Directions:

Mix all together and store in an airtight container.

Gazpacho

If you have leftover tossed salad with a n oil and vinegar based dressing on it, this is a great starter to the salad, and better than throwing out the soggy salad. During a heatwave, just leave the full blender in the fridge and anyone can have quick lunch, or pack a container to eat at school or work.

Ingredients:

1 can condensed tomato soup

2 diced tomatoes

½ cup diced celery

½ cup diced red peppers

½ cup diced green peppers

½ cup diced cucumbers

2 tsp white vinegar

1 tbsp Worcestershire sauce

¼ tsp celery salt

½ tsp salt

¼ tsp pepper

2 tbsp chopped cilantro

water

Directions:

Put it all in a blender. Start to blend slowly. Add water to the desired consistency you like. Another option is to remove a cup or so of the mix while it's still chunky, then puree the rest. Serve the smooth and some chunky together.

Sweet Potato Tater Tots

Tater tots are a standard in school cafeterias. They are crispy little nuggets of potato goodness. Your kids won't feel left out if they bring their own, because these are better and not full of additives and preservatives. Make LOTS!

Ingredients:

2 large peeled sweet potatoes

¼ cup whole wheat flour

¼ cup white flour

1 ½ tsp cinnamon

1 cup panko breadcrumbs

1 egg, whisked

cooking spray

Directions:

Preheat oven to 400°F. Line a baking sheet with non-stick foil or parchment. Boil the potatoes whole until fork tender, drain and cool. Grate the potatoes into a bowl. In another bowl, stir together all the dry ingredients. To make each tot, take a tsp of the potato, shape in your palm, roll in the egg then the dry ingredients. Lay on the sheet. Give them all a quick spray and bake 15 minutes until golden.

Crunchy Chickpea Salad

Make this salad the night before to give the vegetables the chance to soak up the dressing - they get crisp as they pickle slightly in the vinegar. The bright colors make the veggies extra enticing.

Ingredients:

1 can of chickpeas, rinsed and drained

3 cups mixed raw vegetables, cut into small dice, (red, orange and yellow peppers, cucumber, zucchini and summer squash)

1/2 cup chopped fresh parsley

1/2 cup bottled vinaigrette

Directions:

Combine all ingredients in a bowl, toss well and refrigerate overnight.

Extras: Add in some flaked, cooked boneless salmon filet for protein and Omega-3s. Cooked leftover vegetables (asparagus, peas, broccoli) can also be included.

Zucchini and Corn Fritters

Send along a little container of plain Greek yogurt for dipping these.

Ingredients:

1/2 cup milk (or part almond milk is good)

1 tsp white or apple cider vinegar

1 cup whole wheat flour

½ tsp salt

½ tsp baking powder

¼ tsp baking soda

1 egg

2 tsp butter

1 cup thawed frozen corn

1 small zucchini grated

3 tbsp Parmesan cheese

1 sliced green onion

Directions:

Mix it all together like a pancake batter. The zucchini will add moisture. Heat a griddle or skillet and use the butter to cook small fritters 4 at a time. Turn and continue cooking over medium heat until golden and crispy. Store in airtight container for up to a week.

Refrigerator Antipasto

This is the heftiest dip you would ever load onto a chip or cracker. Perfect for hot summer days when a cold lunch is appreciated. Great for picnics.

Ingredients:

¼ cup olive oil

2 cups tiny cauliflower florets

1 diced red pepper

1 diced green pepper

1 cup diced mushrooms

2 cloves chopped garlic

1 cup salsa

2 seeded diced tomatoes

2-3 sliced green onions

1 6oz can flaked drained tuna

½ cup sliced olives (green or black)

salt and pepper to taste

Directions:

Heat the oil and cook the cauliflower, peppers, mushrooms and garlic. Add in all the rest and stir gently so tuna will flake apart. Simmer 10 minutes then cool. Store in containers or mason jars. Keep refrigerated. Serve with salted pita chips, heavy wheat crackers or crostini bread rounds.

Tabouli / Quinoa Salad

If you have vegetarians to feed, sending this in the lunchbox will keep them very happy. Use tabouli which is a bulgur wheat, or quinoa which is a grain that provides a complete protein, or a mixture of both for something unique. Make at least 30 minutes before serving as it really needs to marinate in the flavors before serving.

Ingredients:

1 cup dry quinoa (or bulgur) * Make sure your grain of choice is washed and drained

2 cups water

1 big bunch of flat leaf parsley, finely chopped

½ cup mint leaves

1 English cucumber diced

4 diced tomatoes

½ cup minced red onion

Dressing:

Juice of 2 medium sized lemons

31/4 cup olive oil

½ tsp sea salt

black pepper to taste

¼ tsp cumin

Directions:

Bring 2 cups water to a boil and add the grain. Cook 20 mins and then drain and cool. Chop parsley and mint and combine with vegetables. Make up the dressing in a bowl or shaking jar, then toss in the cooled grain and vegetables. Toss and serve.

Snacks

Anytime Yummies

It's just part of our culture, and our busy lives, to want to eat between meals. It's no different for kids, and most schools have a mid-morning recess break. There's also the time between lunch and dinner, especially that after school time when appetites kick in for a boost. Here are lots of options….take care for nut restricted environments.

Zesty Cheese Straws

These are great for lunchboxes. Make the sticks a little short and they won't be prone to breaking.

Ingredients:

½ cup softened butter

1 pound sharp cheddar at room temp. (227 g stick is ½ lb cheese)

1 ½ cup flour

1 tsp salt

1/4 tsp red pepper

Directions:

Preheat oven to 300°F.

In mixing bowl, cream butter until fluffy. Add cheese until blended. Add flour S&P and mix to form a dough. Chill for 30 mins. Pipe out of a cookie press or form straws or sticks any way you like.

Bake 10-15 min until lightly browned.

Cheese Crisp "Cookies"

These don't last long in the fridge...only because they are great quick snacks and disappear into the lunchboxes. If you want to kick them up, just add more cayenne.

Ingredients:

1 ¾ cup flour

¼ tsp cayenne

Pinch salt

¾ cup butter cut into the dry mixture

Stir in 2 cups rice krispy cereal

2 cups shredded old cheddar

Directions:

Preheat oven to 350°F.

Form I tbsp balls and flatten with a fork on ungreased cookie sheet.

Bake for 20-25 mins.

Make 5 dozen but store airtight.

Fruit Wands and Dip

Fruit kebobs are great for lunchboxes, especially with attached cups of dip. Your kids can make these themselves while you are preparing lunch if you like to involve them .(Take care that some environments don't allow skewers as they can become toys, and unfortunately lead to dangers for little ones.)

Ingredients:

Chunks of fruits –

Melons (cantaloupe, honeydew, firm watermelon)

Grapes, strawberries

Pineapple, orange sections

Apples and pears …squirt with a little lemon to prevent browning

Dips –

Sour cream with a stir in of brown sugar

Pudding cups – any flavor

Cinnamon Crunchies

A great snack choice that's free of additives and artificial flavors. Make up lots because they store so well, and when you put them in a crinkly wrapper, kids think they are like store bought treats.

Ingredients:

1 15 oz. can chickpeas, drained

1/2 tsp ground cinnamon

1 tbsp canola or vegetable oil

1 tbsp honey

Directions:

Preheat oven to 400 F. Line a baking sheet with parchment.

Place the beans between two paper towels and pat dry, loosening the outer skin of the beans. Remove the outer skins of the beans and pat dry to remove any other excess liquid. Whisk the cinnamon and oil in a bowl to combine, add the beans stirring to coat and place on a baking sheet. Roast for 40 minutes.

Remove the beans from the oven, place in a bowl and toss with 1 tbsp of honey. Place the beans back into the oven and roast an additional 7 minutes. Cool completely. Store in a covered container on your counter for up to 2 weeks

Fruit and Seed Bars

These are great for those with nut allergies...or anyone who needs a healthy, satisfying mid-afternoon pick-me-up!

Ingredients:

1 cup dried fruit (blueberries, raisins, currants, cranberries and/or cherries)

1 cup old fashioned oats

1/2 cup raw pumpkin seeds (also known as pepitas)

1/2 cup raw sunflower seeds

2 tablespoons flax seeds

1/2 cup unsweetened coconut flakes

1/3 cup honey

1/2 cup sunflower or almond butter

Directions:

Preheat oven to 325°F. Line a 9" x 9" pan with parchment paper.

In a food processor, pulse the first 6 ingredients until finely chopped (it's ok if there are few coarsely chopped pieces). Add the honey and sunflower and pulse until starting to combine. Pour the mixture into a 9 x 9 inch pan, and press down into the pan until completely even. Bake for 25 minutes. Let the bars completely cool before cutting with a serrated knife into bars.

*Cool, place in Ziploc bags, label and freeze. Defrost to room temperature and enjoy!

Snackin' Snowballs

These are messy to make, but so worth it. Just another place to let kids get involved and get creative.

Ingredients:

1 1/4 cup old fashioned oats, ground in a food processor

1/2 cup peanut butter (you can also use almond, cashew or sunflower butter)

1/2 cup honey

1/2 cup coconut flakes, unsweetened

Directions:

Place the oats in a food processor or blender and pulse until finely ground. Stir the peanut butter and honey in a bowl until thoroughly combined. Add the ground oats and continue to stir until thoroughly combined. Using 1 tsp of the mixture at a time or a mini ice cream scooper to roll into balls. Place the coconut in a separate bowl or plate and roll the balls or logs in the coconut to completely cover.

For freezing: place balls on a sheet tray and freeze for 30 min. Remove, place in a zipper bag, label and place back in freezer. Can be frozen up to 3 months.

Sunshine Muffins

It's always surprising that it takes a whole orange...peel and all, to give these bright and zippy muffins their flavor. Spread with a little cream cheese and they are a very satisfying snack. If you add chocolate chips, be sure to just drop them in at the end as they can fall to the bottom and burn in a loaf.

Ingredients:

1 orange

½ cup orange juice

1 egg

¼ cup vegetable oil

1 ½ cups flour

¾ cup sugar

1 tsp baking powder

1 tsp baking soda

1 tsp salt

½ cup raisins or chocolate cups

½ cup chopped nuts

Directions:

Preheat oven to 375°F. Line a loaf pan with parchment, or paper cups in a muffin tin.

Cut the whole orange into eight or twelve pieces and pop into the blender. Add orange juice, egg and oil and blend until smooth. Mix dry ingredients in a bowl and pour the wet into it then mix together. Add nuts and raisins and pour into 16 muffin tins, or large loaf pan. Bake 25 mins for muffins, and 40 minutes for loaf.

Popcorn Nutty Balls

Popcorn is an inexpensive and healthy snack. But most popcorn balls are loaded with caramelly sugar and preservatives. This option is much better. Roll into balls any size you like and wrap individually in plastic wrap or store in a air tight container.

Ingredients:

1/2 cup almond, sunflower or peanut butter

1/2 cup brown rice syrup

7 cups air popped popcorn

1 tsp vanilla

vegetable oil or spray for handling the balls.

Directions:

Place the nut butter and rice syrup in a saucepan and cook over medium heat until warm, about 1 minute. You don't want the mixture to cook or boil, just loosen up a bit so it becomes spreadable. Pour the mixture over the popcorn in a bowl and with a rubber spatula or using your hands, coat the popcorn with the nut butter mixture.

Take a small portion (a little less than a 1/4 cup) of the popcorn mixture with slightly wet or damp hands and roll into 1 1/2 inch balls. Lay on a sheet until they firm up.

Choco-Banana Flappies

Tortillas are so versatile, and make up quick snacks that hold up well in lunchboxes. Kids will eat them col or at room temperature.

Ingredients:

2 10" whole wheat tortillas

2 tbsps butter, melted

1 medium banana

¼ cup chocolate chips

2 tbsps brown sugar

¼ tsp cinnamon

Directions:

Heat a griddle pan or sandwich press. Spread banana thinly over one tortilla and sprinkle with the chips. Lay other tortilla on top. Brush top with half the butter and half the brown sugar and cinnamon. Spray the pan with cooking spray and lay the tortilla "sandwich" down on sprinkled side. Brush with remaining butter, sugar and cinnamon and grill for 2 -3 minutes on each side. Cool completely and slice into portions.

Chocolate Energy Bars

These are packed with flavors that comes from the roasting of the nuts it can be done in the microwave, in a small skillet or in the oven. But watch, as they can easily burn.

Ingredients:

½ cup shredded coconut

¾ cup chopped dates

½ cups slivered almonds (toasted)

½ cup walnut (toasted)

½ cup raisins

2 tbsps cocoa powder

2 tbsps coconut oil

Directions:

Once toasted nuts are cool, place them in a blender along with coconut and grind coarsely. Remove and set aside.

Add the pitted dates, raisins and cocoa and grind till the mixture comes into a ball. Add the coarsely ground nut mixture and coconut oil to this and blend again till the mixture comes into a ball. It will take a few minutes, but rest your blender in between, scrape and blend for 4 to 5 mins Once done, line small baking tray with parchment. Spread the mixture on to the tray evenly.

With the help of a flat bottomed plate or a bowl, gently press down the mixture to even it out. Refrigerate for about 6 hours to set.

Homemade Animal Crackers

If you can't find tiny cookie cutters, surprisingly play dough cutters come in many small animal shapers. Wash them up and they are ready to use for your own assorted menagerie.

Ingredients:

1 cup shelled sunflower seeds

1/4 cup flax meal

1/4 cup grated coconut (optional. If you don't use coconut, use 1/2 cup flax meal so there is at least 1/2 cup more of dry ingredients.)

1 tbsp honey

Dash of salt

1/4 cup cold water.

Directions:

Preheat oven to 300°F. Place shelled sunflower seeds in a food processor or blender. Grind until texture of coarse meal. Place seed meal into a bowl and add remaining ingredients and stir with a spoon.   Spoon batter onto wax paper. Cover with wax paper and roll out with rolling pin until 1/4-1/8th inch thick. Cut out shapes. Place shapes on greased cookie sheet. Bake for 15 minutes. Remove from oven and cool on wire rack. Delicious served with sweetened yogurt.

Cereal Power Bars

Stock up on cereals when they go on sale. You can play with the mix of cereals if you like, such as brans flakes, rice cereals, wheat squares or oat rings. The more low sugar the better!

Ingredients:

1 2/3 cups cereal

8 dates (chopped, pitted)

1/2 cup coconut

1/2 cup brown sugar

1/2 cup whole wheat flour

1 tsp ground cinnamon

1 can white beans pureed or chopped

1/3 cup honey

3 tbsps melted butter

2 tbsps canola oil

1 tsp vanilla

Dash of salt.

Directions:

Preheat oven to 350°F. Line 13 X 9 pan with foil and spray.

Add dry ingredients plus beans. Mix in wet ingredients. Spread in lined pan. Bake for 30-40 minutes, until edges are browned. Cool completely and cut into bars.

Sammies
and Wraps
Lunchtime one handers

Kids love sandwiches, and they have been a big part of lunchboxes ever since kids starting going to school. But choices and variety have come a long way since the first brown bag options. Don't hesitate to try just about anything your kids like…in a sandwich or a wrap.

Carrot Salad Sandwich

This unexpected sandwich filling is great for incorporating leftovers. The crunch of carrots in a sour-sweet dressing contrast nicely with the rich cream cheese.

Ingredients:

2 slices whole grain bread

1 tablespoon cream cheese, softened

1/3 cup Grated Carrot Salad

Grated Carrot Salad:

3 cups grated carrots (2 to 3 large carrots)

1/4 cup finely chopped fresh Italian (flat) parsley

3 Tbs chopped raisins or sun-dried cranberries or cherries

Salt and ground black pepper

3 Tbs red-wine vinegar

5 Tbs olive oil

Directions:

Divide the cream cheese between the two slices of bread,
spreading thinly to the edges. Spoon the salad evenly onto
one slice of bread and place the second over to cover.
Extras: Grate some cucumber into the salad for color and
juicy crunch.

Corn and Bean Pockets

Tortillas are a great alternative to sliced sandwich bread or buns. The more you work with them the better you get at knowing just how much to fill them. This filling only has four ingredients.

Ingredients:

1/4 cup canned black beans, drained and rinsed

1/4 cup canned corn niblets, drained and rinsed

2 Tbsp. grated cheddar cheese

2 Tbsp. tomato salsa

1 10-inch flour tortilla

Directions:

In a small bowl, combine the beans, corn, cheddar and salsa, stirring to combine. Place filling into the centre of the tortilla. Then roll it up, burrito-style with ends closed, to encase the filling.

Toast, seam side down, in a non-stick pan over medium heat until golden brown. Repeat on other side and refrigerate overnight.

Pulled Chicken Sandwich

Barbecue sauce is a favorite with lots of kids, and this smoky sandwich is sure to be one too.

Ingredients:

1/3 cup shredded skinless cooked chicken

1-1/2 tbsp. barbecue sauce

A few drops apple cider vinegar or water

1 small whole wheat roll

1/3 cup coleslaw (try a vinegar-based one to keep it light)

Directions:

In a small bowl, toss the chicken with half of the barbecue sauce and a few drops of vinegar or water to thin it out. Pile the meat onto a small roll and spoon over the remaining barbecue sauce. Top with the coleslaw.

Inside Out Sandwich Wands

If there's a real jokester in your family, make a surprise out of this lunch idea. Make these inside out sandwiches and they will be sure to get a few giggles.

Ingredients:

4 slices roast turkey

¼ cup cream cheese, softened

¼ cup dried cranberries

4 thick grissini bread sticks, about 6 inches long

1 piece fruit leather, cut into 4 strips

Directions:

Lay a turkey slice on a clean, dry surface. Spread 1 tablespoon cream cheese on it. Sprinkle with 1 tablespoon cranberries.

Lay breadstick across short side of turkey. Roll turkey around breadstick and secure with fruit leather tied in a knot. Repeat.

Banana Cream Cheese Sammies

Ingredients:

2 bananas

4 ounces cream cheese

2 tablespoons nut butter (almond, peanut or cashew work well)

1 1/2 teaspoons honey

1/4 teaspoon cinnamon

Directions:

Mix together nut butter, cream cheese, honey, and cinnamon in a small mixing bowl until creamy. Peel bananas and cut into 1/2 inch slices. Place a dollop of nut butter mixture between two slices and freeze for 30 minutes.

Ham, Cheese and Pear Sandwiches

Ingredients:

4 slices sandwich bread

8 oz. Gruyere cheese

1 pear, thinly sliced

8 oz. deli ham, thinly sliced

Butter

Directions:

Layer 4 slices of sandwich bread with 8 oz Gruyere or other melting cheese, 1 thinly sliced pear, and 8 ounces thinly sliced deli ham; top each with bread.

Heat a large skillet over medium heat. Spread outside of both bread slices with butter. Cook sandwiches in batches, if necessary, until golden and cheese is melted, flipping once, 3 to 5 minutes per side. Cut sandwiches in half and serve hot, or pack off to eat warm from the lunchbox.

Hummus and Veggie Pita

Ingredients:

1 slice whole wheat pita bread

2 tbsp. hummus

1/8 cup feta cheese

1/2 a cucumber, sliced

1/4 cup green onions, chopped

1/4 to 1/2 cup bell peppers

1/3 cup tomatoes, chopped

1/4 cup bean sprouts

1/8 cup carrots, grated

lettuce to taste, whole leaves or shredded

Directions:

Makes at least 4 sandwiches, depending upon how much vegetable filling one prefers.

Any vegetables may be substituted according to taste. Cut, chop, shred, grate or slice vegetables according to preference. Mix all the vegetables together and store them in a plastic container. They'll keep for about 5-7 days, so you have a quick alternative for lunch when I'm in a hurry. The prep time is all in the peeling and cutting when you first make the mixture. You may shred the lettuce and include it at this point, or add whole leaves when you make the sandwich. The lettuce may wilt sooner than the rest of the mixture, so I add it fresh.

When you're ready, spread 2 tbsp. hummus on one slice of pita bread, sprinkle 1/8 c. of feta cheese, and add 1/4 of the vegetable mixture. Fold in half and enjoy.

If you like, you may add a condiment or dressing, or salt and pepper to taste. I like mine just as it is. The bread, hummus, and feta provide enough salt and flavor, and the vegetables are delicious!

Ham and Mustard Spirals

Everybody loves ham and cheese, but a dipping sauce of honey and grainy mustard adds a little spice. Toasting the sandwich crisps the tortilla and makes it easier to chew. This works well with leftover chicken or turkey, too.

Ingredients:

2 tsp. mild grainy mustard

1 tsp. honey

1 10-inch whole wheat tortilla

2 thin slices provolone, Swiss or other cheese that's good for melting

2 slices roasted ham

Directions:

In small container, mix together the mustard and honey. Pack for lunch and set aside. On the tortilla, lay out the two slices of cheese, then the ham on top. Roll, burrito-style, with sides tucked in.

In a nonstick pan over medium heat, toast the roll, seam side down, to seal. Repeat with remaining sides until golden all over. Chill overnight. Serve with chopped vegetables, the dipping sauce and juice. Makes 1-2 servings, depending on age and appetite of child.

Extras: If your kid is more adventurous, pair the roll-up with prepared mango chutney in place of the honey mustard.

Summer Rolls

Rice paper wrappers may be new to your child's diet, but she'll love rolling the filling up herself. They're a breeze to make and completely customizable.

Ingredients:

2 rice paper wrappers

1/3 cup shredded, cooked skinless chicken

1/3 cup shredded cabbage or iceberg lettuce

1/3 cup carrots peeled and cut into thin matchsticks

Directions:

Rehydrate the rice paper wrappers according to the instructions on the package. Lay a small pile of chicken horizontally across the centre of the wrapper, then top with the cabbage and carrot. Roll up, egg roll style (there are often instructions on the package), and chill. Repeat with remaining ingredients. Serve with a small container of your favorite Asian dressing, or some low-sodium soy sauce seasoned with a few drops of lime juice. Fruit and milk complete the meal. Makes 2.

Extras: Sliced cucumber, avocado, seafood can all be used as fillings. Add some grated ginger and garlic to the soy sauce for dipping.

Philly-style Cheesesteak Sammie

Kids with heartier appetites will love this filling combo.

Ingredients:

1 tsp. honey mustard

1 tsp. barbecue sauce

1 10-inch whole wheat tortilla

2 slices low-fat Havarti or other mild melting cheese

2 slices roast beef

1/3 cup roasted mixed peppers

Directions:

Stir together the honey mustard and barbecue sauce, then spread over one third of the tortilla. Over the other two thirds, arrange the cheese, then the beef, then the peppers on top. Roll burrito-style with sides tucked in, to seal.

In a nonstick pan over medium heat, toast the roll seam side down to seal. Repeat with remaining sides until golden all over. Chill overnight.

Buffalo Chicken Wrap

Lovers of buffalo wings will love the combination of flavors in this wrap. Use leftover wing meat if you have it...but wings usually disappear quickly.

Ingredients:

2 tbsps hot pepper sauce, such as Frank's RedHot

3 tbsps white vinegar, divided

1/4 tsp cayenne pepper

2 teaspoons extra-virgin olive oil

1 pound chicken tenders

2 tbsps mayonnaise

2 tbsps nonfat plain yogurt

Freshly ground pepper, to taste

1/4 cup crumbled blue cheese

4 8-inch whole-wheat tortillas

1 cup shredded romaine lettuce

1 cup sliced celery

1 large tomato, diced

Directions:

Whisk hot pepper sauce, 2 tablespoons vinegar and cayenne pepper in a medium bowl. Heat oil in a large nonstick skillet over medium-high heat. Add chicken tenders; cook until cooked through and no longer pink in the middle, 3 to 4 minutes per side. Add to the bowl with the hot sauce; toss to coat well.

Whisk mayonnaise, yogurt, pepper and the remaining 1 tablespoon vinegar in a small bowl. Stir in blue cheese. To assemble wraps: Lay a tortilla on a work surface or plate. Spread with 1 tablespoon blue cheese sauce and top with one-fourth of the chicken, lettuce, celery and tomato. Drizzle with some of the hot sauce remaining in the bowl and roll into a wrap sandwich. Repeat with the remaining tortillas.

Sweet Treats

Tasty finishing touches

We all know that kids love sweets (and they are not the only ones!). These easy and mouthwatering treats will satisfy the sweetest of teeth. Yum yum.

Healthy Whoopie Pies

A dark chocolatey pie is what makes a whoopie pie so distinctive...and these are made extra dark, rich and delicious with the addition of pureed beets. Moist and nutritious...enjoy the indulgence.

Ingredients:

½ cup cocoa powder

2 cups flour

1 ½ tsp baking powder

¼ tsp salt

1/3 cup oil

3 eggs

1 ¼ cup sugar

1 ½ cup pureed beets

1 tsp vanilla

Directions:

Preheat oven to 350°F. line baking sheets with parchment.. Sift together the dry ingredients. In a separate bowl, beat sugar, eggs and oil. Add wet to dry and combine and stir in the beats. Drop on parchment in mounds of one tablespoon. Bake 10 minutes and will be slightly cracked on the top.

Filling:

2 tbsp softened butter

3 tbsps marshmallow topping

1 cup icing sugar

1-2 tbsps milk.

Mix together and spread filling between two whoopie cakes to make whoopie pies.

Karrot's Cake

This is such a versatile cake that it can be used as muffins, a loaf, a layer cake or a great sheet cake for parties and functions. It freezes so well that it is easy to keep ready to go in the freezer for any occasion.

Ingredients:

½ cup brown sugar

½ cup white sugar

3 eggs

1 cup white flour

½ cup whole wheat pastry flour

2 cups grated carrots

½ tsp salt

1 1/3 tsps baking soda (that's right)

1 ½ tsp cinnamon

½ tsp cloves

½ cup chopped nuts

½ cup raisins

½ cup drained crushed pineapple

Directions:

Preheat oven to 300°F prepare pan of choice (13 x 9, or 2 8" round with parchment paper or muffin pan with 24 muffin papers). Beat together oil and sugar. Add eggs one at a time and beat after each. Mix in dry ingredients until well blended. Fold in raw carrots, nuts, raisins and pineapple. Pour into 9x13 greased pan. Bake 300°F for 1 hour – or 2 layers for 40 mins.

Cranberry Oat Cereal Bars

Cranberries add so much tart and sweet flavor to any treat. Stock up when they go on sale...and try the new flavored cranberries that many bulk stores off.

Ingredients:

Nonstick cooking spray

4 tablespoons unsalted butter

1 bag (10 ounces) marshmallows

1/2 teaspoon salt

6 cups toasted oat cereal

1 cup dried cranberries, or raisins

Directions:

Melt the butter and marshmallows in a large microwaveable bowl, about 1 minute. They will puff up when you take them out of the oven, so stir them a little until they fall Stir in the rest and move it quickly. Pat the mixture evenly onto a cookie sheet and refrigerate. Cut in to bars.

Blueberry Cheesecake Bites

It seems that anything that ends up in a paper muffin cup is suitable for a lunchbox. Dessert sizes are controlled, and fresh fruit can be used for the toppings when it is in season.

Ingredients:

18 vanilla wafers

4 ounces cream cheese at room temperature

1 large egg

1 tsp vanilla

¼ cup sour cream

1/3 cup brown sugar

1 cup blueberries (strawberries, raspberries)

Directions:

Preheat oven to 300°F. Line a muffin tin with 18 liners. Place one vanilla wafer cookie in each muffin paper. Beat together the cheese, egg, vanilla, sugar and sour cream. Fold in the fruit and spoon over each vanilla wafer. Bake 45-50 minutes. Cool and serve.

Healthy Oatmeal Cookies

Keep these soft and chewy , or cook a little longer for those who like a crispy cookie for dipping into a glass of milk or a hot beverage.

Ingredients:

½ cup white flour

½ cup whole wheat flour

1 tsp baking powder

2/3 cup brown sugar

1/3 cup canola oil

1 egg

1 tsp vanilla

½ cup rolled oats

½ cup dried currants or raisins

Directions:

Preheat oven to 350°F. Line cookie sheets with parchment paper. Mix together the dry ingredients. Beat in the oil and egg, and vanilla. Stir in the oats and currants. Drop by teaspoonful onto parchment and bake 15 minutes. Cool.

Chocolate Zucchini Cake

Ingredients:

1/2 cup (1 stick) unsalted butter, melted and cooled

1 cup sugar

1 large egg

24 walnut halves

1 cup all-purpose flour

1 cup finely grated zucchini (from 1 medium zucchini)

1/4 cup unsweetened cocoa powder

1/2 cup (3 ounces) bittersweet chocolate, chopped, or chocolate chips

3 tablespoons sour cream

1/2 teaspoon coarse salt

1/2 teaspoon pure vanilla extract

Nonstick cooking spray

Directions:

Preheat oven to 350°F. Line a 9" x 9" pan with parchment paper.

Cream butter and sugar together with medium speed mixer. Add egg and beaten until incorporated. Stir in all the rest, in order, one at a time. Pour into the pan. Bake 25-30 minutes.

Gingersnaps

A favorite dipper for a hot drink, or to take them along on a hike or walk. If you like them with a little more pepperiness, take the ginger quantity up a few notches.

Ingredients:

2/3 cup canola oil

1 1/a cups turbinado sugar,

1 large egg

4 tablespoons molasses

2 cups sifted whole-wheat pastry flour

2 teaspoons baking soda

1 1/4 teaspoons ground cinnamon

1 1/4 teaspoons ground ginger…or more

1/4 teaspoon sea salt

¼ cup turbinado sugar

Directions:

Preheat oven to 350°F. Line two baking sheets with parchment paper. Beat the egg and add in the oil, sugar and then molasses. Stir in the dry ingredients. Refrigerate the dough about 30 mins. Roll into 1 " balls. Press each down on the sheet and sprinkle with the sugar. Babe 10-12 minutes until edges are golden and appear crispy.

Quick and Easy PopTarts

Refrigerator pie pastry in a roll is a great product to keep on hand. It keeps for weeks and is so easy to handle. Make your poptarts in any shape you like...especially around holiday times.

Ingredients:

1 package refrigerator pie crust

1 egg yolk

water

fruit jam, any flavour

turbinado or raw sugar

Directions:

Preheat oven to 400°F. Line a cookie sheet with parchment paper. Work on a flour dusted surface. Open out pastry and decide on shapes on half. Spoon 1 tbsp of jam into the middle of each shape and top with identical shape. Press edges together with a fork. Whisk egg and water together.

Use this "glue" painted on the edges and a little over the top. Bake 10-12 minute until browned

Chocolate Fudge Pop Tarts

Who doesn't love pop tarts? That's why these will be a sure winner.

Ingredients:

3 1/2 cups flour (mix whole wheat, coconut, almond and white)

3 tbsps unsweetened cocoa powder

1 tbsp sugar

1/2 tsp salt

 (3/4 cup) cold cubed butter

1/2 cup ice cold water

Fudge Filling

1/4 cup unsweetened cocoa powder

1/3 cup packed brown sugar

2/3 cup milk (or heavy cream)

1/4 tsp salt

6 oz milk chocolate, chopped

2 tbsps cubed cold butter

2 tsp vanilla

Frosting

2 cups icing sugar

2 tbsps meringue powder

1 tbsp vanilla

2 tbsps cocoa powder

3-6 tbsps water

2 oz dark or milk chocolate, melted

coarse sugar, for sprinkling

Directions:

Preheat the oven to 400° F. Line a baking sheet with parchment paper. Start with fudge filling. Stir together cocoa, sugar, milk , salt and half of the chopped milk chocolate in a small sauce pan and cook over medium heat, stirring, until chocolate is melted. Cook mixture at a low boil, stirring occasionally for 5 minutes. Remove pan from heat, add remaining chocolate, butter and vanilla and stir until smooth. Set aside to cool and thicken.

For the pastry combine the flour, cocoa powder, sugar and salt in a large mixing bowl. Add chunks of the butter and mix with a pastry blender or your fingers until the mixture is crumbly. Gradually add the water until the mixture is moistened and a dough forms. Place the dough in between two large sheets of parchment paper or on a lightly floured surface and roll out into an 1/8-inch thickness, using the parchment paper or working on a lightly floured surface.

Cut the dough into rectangles, about 6 1/2 x 4 1/2 inches. Place a heaping tablespoon of filling on one half of the rectangle. Lay the other half of the dough over the filling and seal the edges by crimping with the back of a fork. Repeat until all the dough has been used, saving the scraps and re-rolling to make more rectangles.

Bake the pop tarts for 10 to 12 minutes. Cool completely

While the pop tarts cool make the frosting. In the bowl of stand mixer, mix the icing sugar, meringue powder, vanilla, cocoa powder and 3 tablespoons water for about 7-10 minutes on medium speed, until peaks begin to form. Stir in the melted chocolate. If your frosting seems too thick, thin as needed for outlining or flooding by adding more water. About 5 tablespoons of water works.

Spoon a thin layer of the frosting on top of cooled pop tarts. Allow frosting to harden 10 minutes and then if desired sprinkle with course sugar. Place on a baking sheet and allow the tarts to harden uncovered, about 2 hours.

Granola Balls

You'll be a big hit when these show up in the lunchbox, but send extra because they will end up traded or shared.

Ingredients:

2 cups quick oats

1 cup crispy rice cereal

1 cup creamy peanut butter

1 cup ground flaxseed

1 cup mini chocolate chips

2/3 cup honey or agave nectar

2 teaspoons pure vanilla extract

2 tablespoons coconut oil

Directions:

Combine all the ingredients together in a large bowl, mixing gently so the crispy rice cereal doesn't get crushed. Mix until well-combined.

Using a cookie scoop (or roll small amounts in your hands), drop rounded tablespoonful-sized portions onto a parchment or wax paper lined cooking sheet. I used my cookie scoop and then rolled the scooped portion out between my palms.

Refrigerate for 1-2 hours. At this point you can serve them or combine the chilled granola bites in a large air tight container or zipper bags to freeze or refrigerate. They will stay fresh in the refrigerator for up to a week or for a few months in the freezer.

Gluten Free
Options
For Everyone

Gluten free foods are necessary for people who suffer with Celiac Disease, but they are becoming more and more mainstream as it becomes apparent that grain products are contributors to belly fat and weight issues. Luckily on the market today is a wide assortment of flour alternatives. Start playing with them and their quantities and you will soon find textures and combinations that work for many of your favorite recipes.

Chocolate Chickpea Cake

This is great lunchbox cake. It is so moist that it doesn't need a frosting. Fresh fruit , particularly berries, work well as a topper.

Ingredients:

19 oz can chickpeas

4 eggs

¾ cup sugar

1 ½ cup chocolate chips melted

½ tsp baking powder

icing sugar for dusting

Directions:

Preheat oven to 350° degrees. Line a 9" round pan with parchment, or use a spring form pan.

Pulse chickpeas in food processor. Don't completely puree, but leave chunky. Add sugar and eggs and mix. Melt chocolate chips in microwave until just melted. Combine. Pour into the pan. Bake for 40 minutes. While warm dust with icing sugar. Use a doily laid over top for a pretty stencil.

Coconut Flour Orange Cake

Preheat oven to 350°F. Melt the coconut oil in a 8" x 8" square pan in the oven, spread it around and let it cool.

Ingredients:

6 eggs

1/4 cup coconut oil

1/4 cup coconut milk

6 tbsps honey

1 tsp vanilla extract

1/2 tsp orange zest

1/2 cup coconut flour

1/2 tsp baking powder

1/2 tsp sea salt

juice of 1/2 medium orange

Directions:

Take your eggs out of your refrigerator and allow them to come to room temperature. Whisk the eggs, coconut milk, honey, vanilla and orange zest together. Combine coconut flour, baking powder and sea salt. Stir the dry ingredients into the wet. Spread the oil all around the pan to coat evenly, then pour remainder of the coconut oil into the batter and mix until all lumps are gone.

Pour the batter into your greased pan and place on the middle rack of the oven. Bake for 35-40 minutes, until browned on top and a toothpick comes out clean. Place the cake on a cooling rack. After the cake has cooled a bit, but is still warm, poke holes all over the top with a fork. Juice the orange half right over the whole cake, making sure to evenly distribute the juice.

Orange Coconut Oil Frosting

Ingredients:

1/2 cup coconut oil, melted in a glass bowl

9 drops of liquid stevia, or 2 packets Splenda (or a couple of teaspoons of raw honey)

1 packed teaspoon orange zest

1/2 teaspoon vanilla extract

pinch of salt

Directions:

Mix all ingredients into warm coconut oil. You are now going to place the bowl into the freezer in order to cool it down. It is very important to check on it every couple of minutes to catch it before it gets too cold. You want to take it out of the freezer right when it starts to get cloudy.

At this point the cold bowl (and your cool kitchen) will continue to turn the liquid oil into a solid. Continue to whisk the frosting as it gets cloudier and cloudier and eventually turns into a whipped butter consistency. The idea is to get a bit of air into it. Once it is to a whipped (very soft) butter consistency plop it onto your cooled cake. Frost it very quickly before the coconut oil hardens. It will seem like a pretty thin layer of frosting, but it is just enough.

Jumbo Muffins

There's so many other flavors going on in these muffins that the combination of flours is very disguised.

Ingredients:

1 cup oats

1 cup milk

1/3 cup brown sugar

¼ cup melted butter

…mix and let sit

1 cup mixed flours (2/3 rice, 1/3 tapioca and potato)

½ tsp salt

½ tsp xanthan gum

½ tsp baking soda

1 ½ baking powder

½ cup chopped nuts (½ cup shredded carrot nice option)

½ cup coconut

½ cup raisins

½ tsp cinnamon

½ tsp nutmeg

Directions:

Preheat oven to 375°F. Line muffin pan with paper liners. Mix oats, milk, sugar and oil together. Mix dry ingredients and then bring the two together. Add two beaten eggs and stir everything together. Pour into muffin cups and bake 15-20 mins until golden.

Chicken Asparagus Crepes

These crepes are great to make ahead and then fill with any gluten-free choices you have on hand. Leftover chicken and any vegetables are great favorites with kid's appetites.

Ingredients:

Crepe mix:

1 tbsp butter, melted

1 tbsp gluten free flour

1 egg

3/4 cup skim milk

1/8 teaspoon nutmeg

16 asparagus spear, with woody end removed

1 oz Swiss cheese, shredded

1 cup cooked shredded chicken

4 sliced green onion

bottled Caesar salad dressing

juice of one lemon

Directions:

Steam or part-cook the asparagus to medium crispness. Meanwhile, whip together the crepe mix and set aside. Heat a medium frying or crepe pan and coat with cooking spray. Pour 1 ½ tbsp batter into the centre of pan, turn all over to create a crepe, cook until firm, then flip and cook until edges crisp. Make 4-5 crepes this way and col on a plate.

To assemble, lay 2 spears asparagus, ¼ cup chicken, a few slices of green onion and a dribble of dressing, squirt of lemon juice on each, fold end and roll. Store in refrigerator until ready to send off for lunch.

Rice Noodle Salad

Rice noodles are a great alternative to pasta. Make up a double batch of this favorite salad and serve cold to your cold lunch fans, or warm it up in the microwave before popping it into the lunchbox so it will be still warm at lunchtime.

Ingredients:

250 g medium rice noodles

85 g sundried tomatoes plus 2 tbsp of their oil

1 tbsp slivered celery

1 small carrot grated

2 sliced green onions

3 garlic cloves

25g Parmesan shaved or grated

large handful basil leaves, torn

Directions:

Prepare the noodles according to pack instructions, then drain. Heat the oil, then fry the tomatoes, celery, carrot and garlic for 3 mins. Toss the noodles and most of the cheese and basil into the pan, season, then scatter over the remaining cheese and basil. Works well served at room temperature.

Tuna, Asparagus and White Bean Salad

Full of flavors and fab for your insides.

Ingredients:

1 large bunch asparagus

2 x 200g cans tuna in water, drained

2 x 400g cans cannellini beans in water, drained

1 red onion, very finely chopped

2 tbsp capers

1 tbsp olive oil

1 tbsp red wine vinegar

2 tbsp tarragon, finely chopped

Directions:

Cook the asparagus in a large pan of boiling water for 4-5 mins until tender. Drain well, cool under running water, then cut into finger-length pieces. Toss together the tuna, beans, onion, capers and asparagus in a large serving bowl.

Mix the oil, vinegar and tarragon together, then pour over the salad. Chill until ready to serve.

Coconut Curry Noodle Bowl

Noodles bowls are a great easy lunch for all ages, as long as you adjust the heat level for your less adventurous appetites. Keep a batch in the fridge to serve up into thermal bottles or containers for the fans of cold noodle dishes.

Ingredients:

2 cups vegetable broth

1 small jalapeño, seeded and finely minced

2 garlic cloves, minced

1 tbsp curry powder (or 1 tbsp red or green Thai curry paste)

14 oz (1 box) unsweetened coconut milk

1 cup unsweetened soy or almond milk

1 tsp salt

2 tsps freshly grated ginger

1/2 lb rice vermicelli noodles, cooked

1 cup chicken cooked

2 small tomatoes, cored and cut into 1-inch chunks

3 tbsps fresh lime juice

1/3 cup chopped fresh cilantro

Directions:

Simmer the vegetable broth with the jalapeno and garlic. Start adding the rest, in order and simmer until flavors are incorporated.

Chewy Macaroons

The key to making macaroons chewy and moist is to use a full fat coconut for this recipe. It's the full fat that holds the dough together so the cookies won't be too dry.

Ingredients:

1/3 cup of egg whites from 2 extra large eggs,

3/4 cup sugar (5 1/2 oz, 150g)

2 - 2 1/4 cups medium grate unsweetened coconut

5 teaspoons smooth, unsweetened applesauce (regular or baby food)

If you want a crunchy cookie surface with lots of crevasses, use 2 1/4 cups. If you want a more smooth cookie surface, use 2 cups.

Directions:

Preheat oven to 425°F. Line a baking sheet with parchment. Place the unsweetened coconut in a food processor. Pulse for 60 seconds. Combine the egg whites, sugar, coconut, and applesauce in a medium-sized, thick-bottomed saucepan. Mix well and heat on medium low heat, stirring frequently, until the ingredients are well incorporated, and the mixture forms a smooth paste and is warm to the touch (about 120°F). If the mixture seems too dry or stiff to pipe through a piping bag, add a little more applesauce. If the mixture seems too wet, add a little more coconut.

Place warm mixture into a pastry bag and pipe tall mounds onto a baking sheet, about an inch and a half apart from each other. Or form mounds with a 1 tablespoon sized scoop. Let the formed cookies dry out for a few minutes (15 minutes or so) before baking.

Bake the cookies until they start to get color on the edges where the cookie meets the pan, 5 to 7 minutes. Let cool on the pan for a couple minutes, then carefully lift the pan liner with the cookies off the pan and place on a rack. The cookies will firm up as they cool. Once cool, remove from the pan liner.

Store in a covered box for up to 5 days at room temperature.

Thanks For Reading.

Parents really are the superheroes and true champions of the universe.

Mum, dad, I salute you!

Have a beautiful and tasty day.

Made in the USA
Las Vegas, NV
18 August 2023

76251353R00132